A Flower Whose Name I Do Not Know

The National Poetry Series

The National Poetry Series was established in 1978 to publish five collections of poetry annually through five participating publishers: Persea Books, William Morrow & Co., the University of Illinois Press, Copper Canyon Press, and Viking Penguin. The manuscripts are selected by five poets of national reputation. Publication is funded by the Copernicus Society of America, James A. Michener, Edward J. Piszek, and the Lannan Foundation.

1991

GOOD HOPE ROAD, by Stuart Dischell
    Selected by Thomas Lux, Viking Penguin.

THE DIG, by Lynn Emanuel
    Selected by Gerald Stern, the University of Illinois Press.

TO PUT THE MOUTH TO, by Judith Hall
    Selected by Richard Howard, William Morrow & Co.

AS IF, by James Richardson
    Selected by Amy Clampitt, Persea Books.

A FLOWER WHOSE NAME I DO NOT KNOW,
    by David Romtvedt
    Selected by John Haines, Copper Canyon Press.

D0359323

COPPER CANYON PRESS

PORT TOWNSEND

A Flower

Whose Name

I Do Not Know

POEMS BY

David

Romtvedt

THE NATIONAL POETRY SERIES

SELECTED BY JOHN HAINES

Thanks to the following magazines in whose pages some of these poems appeared: *The Arts* (newsletter of the King County Arts Commission), *Bumbershoot Anthology*, *Calliope*, *Cincinnati Poetry Review*, *Columbia*, *Crab Creek Review*, *Dalmo'ma*, *Die Young*, *Earth's Daughters*, *Elf*, *Event* (Canada), *Hampden-Sydney Poetry Review*, *Hubbub*, *Luna Tack*, *Memphis State Review*, *MSS*, *Open Places*, *Raccoon*, *Seattle Voice*, *Soundings*, *South Florida Poetry Review*, *Stone Drum*, *The Sun*, and *Tidepools*.

"Bamboo" was published by the Blue Begonia Press in *Cotton Nails*, a poetry portfolio, and as a broadside to benefit the Hood Canal Peace Blockade of the first Trident submarine in August of 1982.
Black Beauty and Kiev, the Ukraine was published as a chapbook by the Blue Begonia Press to benefit the Ground Zero Center for Non-Violent Action.
"Guatemala, the Year of Our Lord 1984" was published by Empty Bowl in the anthology *In Our Hearts and Minds: The Northwest and Central America*, and in the anthology *80 on the 80's*.
The author would like to thank the UCross Foundation for a residency during which some of these poems were written, and the National Endowment for the Arts for a fellowship which supported this work.

Copper Canyon Press is in residence with Centrum at Fort Worden State Park.
Copper Canyon Press receives financial support from the Washington State Arts Commission.
The type in this book is Janson. Composition by The Typeworks, Vancouver, B.C.

Library of Congress Cataloging-in-Publication Data
Romtvedt, David.
    A flower whose name I do not know / David Romtvedt.
      p.   cm.
    I S B N 1-55659-046-6
    I. Title.
PS3568.O5655F56   1992
811'.54—dc20   92-8819

COPPER CANYON PRESS
P.O. Box 271, Port Townsend, Washington 98368

Contents

For my mother Borgny
and my sister Laura

———————————

Shelter

When I was a boy the neighbor
across the street built a bomb shelter
for three thousand dollars. One evening
while watering his lawn he told my father
about the air filter and chemical toilet,
the water purification system and dried food.
He said in a nuclear war all of us
would come running to him, begging
to be let into his shelter. But he'd be firm.
There was room for only his family. If others
tried to force their way in, he'd shoot them.

There in the yard I pretended to play
with some stinkbugs on a mulberry tree
and run around in the fading heat, but really
I listened. My father said nothing.
Like others, he wanted to protect his family.
But who could tell if a hole in the ground would?
And even I knew he didn't have three thousand dollars.

Sometimes in the summer, after I'd gone to bed,
when the air was still very warm, the neighbor
would go outside and fire his rifle at the stars.
The sound of the shot came through the walls
of my room. I closed my eyes and saw
the bomb shelter we didn't have.

My father outfitted our bathroom with a box
of canned soups and large jars of water.
Sitting on the toilet I faced the box

and wondered how a bathroom could be a bomb shelter.
Twice we all went in there together to practice.
We turned out the light and tried not to collide.
Mama slept in the bathtub, Papa on the floor
beneath the sink, Sister and I, facing each other,
our legs tucked behind the toilet bowl.
Time passed and we forgot our precautions. One day
the water and canned soups were gone. But even now
when I sit on a toilet I see that stuff. And when I hear
a sharp noise, it's the neighbor shooting the stars.

Black Beauty, a Praise

On August 12, 1982, the first Trident-class submarine, the USS Ohio, passed through the Straits of Juan de Fuca and into Admiralty Inlet on its way to its Hood Canal home port at Bangor, Washington. A non-violent Peace Blockade of about fifty people in small rowboats attempted to meet, greet and stop the Ohio. The Peace Blockade was turned back by ninety-eight Coast Guard vessels sent to protect the submarine.

*

In sub-Saharan Africa, praise poems are composed to honor a generous superior, the attributes of an admired animal, a natural event, a technological innovation like the bicycle or the railroad train, or the author's valor. Clever cow thieves sometimes compose praises to themselves. Since the penalty for cattle thievery is immediate death, anyone who gets away with it is generally allowed a little self-praise. Words of praise are like water, like rain on manioc. They call for celebrating. Usually there is dancing to accompany praising – high stepping followed by sudden crouching, pirouetting to take aim at some distant phantasmal creature. Sometimes praising is done in a closed hut and the singer's friends will fire off rifles loaded with blanks. The shots resound off the tin roof. The room fills with smoke. Most listeners flee to the porch, choking. But the singer keeps on singing, staring intently through the smoke, singing praises. One who is really good can keep it up for hours.

*

Oh, dark Trident of the Electric Boat Yard, risen from your technological womb in Groton, Connecticut and dressed in steel, there you are, Black Beauty disguised as an Outlaw God or sinking angel, greetings, and

Praise as you enter the Inland Waters, the realm of the 10,000 clouds, the home of the tongues of Ish, the protector of various birds. Now you come, pushing foam before your prow. Our farmers lie down in their fields, our fishermen spill their nets back into the sea, the glittering gills of the fish reflect light onto your dark surface,

Praise to you, and

Praise to him who takes you below for you do not sink alone, God though you are, you are taken below by men who, even out of sight, remain fully clothed.

Praise to the golden embroidery on their hats and sleeves, the rainbow bars on their shirt fronts, the rich woolen pants that warm their legs in the perpetual cool night on board,

Praise to electric lights,

Praise to the light switches,

Praise to the bulbs' brilliant glow,

Praise to everything on board and greetings Navyman, you drive all over the world, into the sea's deepest caverns where even the moon's coldest light cannot reach, from Vladivostok to San Diego you go,

Praise to your very quiet motors which your enemies cannot hear, for your way is silent, to greet all peoples equally and surprise them. When you shift gears and the delicate clunk rises to the surface, you beg pardon of the insects and birds and in so doing,

Praise them, the fish, the Orca in their pods, the honeybees in late fall
stumbling from monkshood to nasturtium, the crane flies clat-
tering through the air in what to a human eye seems drunken de-
light, the black cormorants resting on your tower, invisible,

Praise, Trident class submarine Ohio, elder brother to Michigan and
Florida, those watery states,

Praise to all holders of rapid deployment death,

Praise to the stalking of death. Like the hunter who hunts not for the
meat but for the sport, so you patrol the infinite drops of water,
aware that both meat and death are at home, or at the butcher's.

Praise to your chore which is to have no chore. Only you, most pow-
erful thing men have made, can wait this way with nothing to
do, resisting boredom and error, only you, in the darkest green
of the deepest hidden pool, at rest, testing your hatches and
springs, assured no rivet will pop, taking your ease,

Praise. Far above you on the surface of the water is a tiny orange
boat – exterior shop-grade plywood – also waiting. A man and
woman sit in it,

Praise to these people of the eternally damp hair, hands wrinkled, skin
soft and pale, small

Praise to them and to their small boat. And greetings too, for they
have come to meet you, to wave their hands and offer loaves of
bread wrapped in plastic, and stop and keep you.

Praise to bread kept safe from the sea, seaweed all around and edible
fish, gulls, mountains which come down to the sea, mountains
becoming the sea.

Praise to the ninety-eight boats of the Coast Guard come to clear your
    way, like a farmer who hacks down brambles with a machete to
    clear the way to an abandoned outhouse.

Praise to the red stripes on the Coast Guard boats,

Praise to the diesel smoke and fumes, helicopters in the sky, water
    cannons, fifty caliber machine guns, M-16's and 45's and confu-
    sion, TV newspeople, Australians, Canadians, Americans, Pa-
    cific Islanders with no country but home and almost no home
    left to go to,

Praise.

Praise to community, as together we carry out this non-task, this
    withholding of power. For if you fire, and the world we praise
    explodes, and the trees shudder and fall under a hot sun and
    even the local wood rats are irradiated, then you fail,

Praise. But if somehow under some other human sun the world burns
    and you open your doors in anger, greetings, and your MIRVed
    missiles are given the gift of flight, then again,

Praise, you fail, and we do, too. So greetings to us all and

Praise, we're damp, ten thousand clouds in the sky, the tongues of the
    people cut out, hungry gull crying in the wake,

Praise, and Navyman, take her down,
                take her deep,
                take her away.

A Flower Whose Name I Do Not Know

Luminous three-foot leaves
float across an ocean of darkness,
a shimmering face with numberless eyes
that open and close.

The yellow sun, the black sky.
I can feel the tension
as each tries to erase the other.

The city clicks and hums
but the cloud overhead passes
as if over a fallow field.

The air is the same air
I breathed in Paradise
and Buchenwald.

A beautiful perfumed woman
enters the room. I want to stare
at her legs but her scent
is so strong it burns my nose.

I stand up to walk away.
As I open the door
I am slapped in the face
by another world
and it is this one.

The Aspen from the Mountain

The world is so close it almost touches us.
We do not know if it is beautiful. It turns.
The leaves of the trees rattle in the rolling.
The clouds and rain rise next to our faces.

The common birds are magpie and eagle and crow,
large birds able to fly into strong winds.
Their feathers lift up spiky and tough.
They can fly to other planets
and find food wherever they go.

Wherever they go, I think, and that thought
passes wistfully, my dream of flight.
The birds sit in the trees.

In my family, it is my mother who can both fly
and sit. She is at her desk writing a letter
to a sister or brother or cousin or niece.
How many thousands of these letters she has written.
She tells about the weather and church and meals
eaten or missed and births and deaths and marriages.
She tells the important news again and again.

Together we drove up the mountain, then walked
past spruce and pine and fir to the aspen,
frail thin leafless sticks.
I dug a large circle around each one, then under,

wanting to make sure we would not injure the roots.
We lifted two trees from the earth and set them
in the back of the pickup. Down the mountain
we planted the trees in our yard. There they are.
A crow stands on a leafless branch,
bending it almost to the ground.

To Make It Now

Grandma stands in the kitchen, still alive.
Her first man died in the twenties,
forty years later the second went the same way.
She stays alive so we celebrate
another birthday, halfway through
her eighties the year I turn thirty.
On the lawn her second son plays volleyball
with his own grown children.
Her eldest son, my father, watches
and makes loud jokes. Like we expect
when we come to this city, it rains.
Everyone plays on, slightly damp.
Later there is a kind of horseshoes
with giant darts and a plastic ring.
We eat heavy American food and sit
in lawn chairs or on benches
at borrowed tables. One grandson
brings his two children but not their mother.
The aunts call him brave
to raise these children by himself,
a man alone. Grandma loves
her great-grandchildren, their tiny eyes
and hands. All afternoon she drinks
bourbon and water. I have made my retreat
to the kitchen where I wash dishes.
My aunt thanks me. Of course
it is I who must give thanks.
Grandma comes in wanting another drink,
aware that now some whisper
she shouldn't. But why not, she asks,

"Why shouldn't an old lady drink if she wants?"
She tells me I am good
and wonders if I think it bad
she drinks. I have no answer
but I pour out more bourbon
and wash more dishes. She comes close
to me and puts her arm in mine.
How odd that I would grow up
a poet. My mother has shown her a poem
for my other grandmother, dead
fifteen years before. "A lovely poem,"
she says, "I had to read it twice.
I didn't understand at first how a woman
could be a bird or tree – then
the second time I saw what you meant."
I am grateful to her for this
and we are quiet. With so many people
there are plenty of dishes.
Then she says my name, tells me
she too would like a poem,
that would be something. Grandma
sets her glass on the counter
asking if I can write a poem
before a person is dead?
I rinse the soap off my hands
and promise I will.

Crossing a Wide Flat Place

Cross-country skiing
through the bright cold night,
I can't get my friend Elena
out of my mind, the Salvadoran clinic
where she works and the sick children
she sees each day.
It is a beautiful night –
the moon is rising,
the sky remains blue,
though it is heavy with darkness.
Michelle skis ahead of me.
There is a rocking motion
to her body; it rises and falls.
Her knees thrust forward,
her hardened thighs stretch,
her arms go up like smoke.
We ski far and fast
so that even in the cold
I feel damp and warm,
and think again of Elena
and the children,
the warmth of their breath
in the heat where they lie,
their arms pressed tightly
to their sides.
Michelle slips over a hill,
deep into Okanagan woods.
It is so warm
she's taken off her mittens
and pushed up her sleeves.
Her body leans ahead,

probing the air like a surgeon
entering the cavity of a body.
We've tried to reach Elena,
calling on the phone,
but she's never home.
Her friend, whom we've not met,
seems alarmed. This thing,
she says, *Esta cosa*.
I do not know where she has gone.
No sé a donde fue.
Like leaf and fall, Elena
is there and then she is not.
Among aspen and lodgepole pine,
an owl crosses the flat earth.
At the bottom of a hill
a coyote and her pups howl.
The pups vibrate
like frayed strings.
Now we are crossing
a wide flat place.
I pass Michelle, gray
wool hat pushed back
on her head and her skis
now like this, now like that.
The snow crystals melting
under her make a shhh,
shhh sound as they turn
to water. It is Elena's
voice, asking, "Can you
send more blood? For
transfusions. There is
never enough." I turn
and ask Michelle, "Did you
hear something?" "Only
a magpie." she tells me.

"Did you?" Yes.
My skis have iced up.
The Salvadoran heat.
We go on. Each tree,
each bush, I know them
by name. I stretch out
a pole and strike a silver
sage. It sways then returns.
Snow falls from the thin leaves.
It could snow tonight.
Even though it's a warm night,
it could snow. "Warm night,"
Michelle whispers, and I believe
she heard Elena's voice,
but I can't ask outright.
Shhh, shhh is the sound
our skis make over snow,
and the sound coyote pups
make beside their mother,
and the sound of a pygmy owl
leaving a tree. All these
voices crossing in the air.
Dear Elena, can we call the world
just? If we could call the world
barely just, could you
somehow get more blood?
I whisper Elena's name,
tell her I will do what I can,
skiing in the night.
Can you hear us, Elena?
Shhh, shhh, our bodies
over the snow, shhh, shhh,
the wooden slats we wear
on our feet, shhh,
shhh, like a broom sweeping
the earth, shhh, shhh, shhh.

In Winter

FOR LISE PETRICH

This time of year the sun comes up
later and goes down earlier.
It doesn't matter. We're making
money; we're trying to make
friends. We fall in love again
and again. Today I'm cleaning up
the garden, tearing out mushy
nasturtiums, storing away bean poles,
turning over the earth. The new
crop of peas is in flower but
I don't know if there will be fruit,
last night the frost. When
your bus stalls on Greenwood Avenue,
making that last climb up to home,
throw a scarf around your neck
and step down onto the city street,
begin the walk and if you think,
as the traffic moves, that something
is wrong, don't let on.
We get what we ask for
though maybe we don't ask
often enough. And everywhere
we are, there is a person
somewhere else for whom we live
in memory. These few notes
are greetings to honor the night,
the winter, the rain as it touches
the ground, and you.

On a Warm Summer Evening
I Sit Reading a Book of Zen

A blast of thunder and then hot rain,
each drop a vast single circle on the earth.
The point is the rain leaving the sky
and the perfect circle disappearing
into the dust. Tired of reading,

I look up and see my neighbor
cutting his grass with an electric mower,
the bright orange cord a snake through the green.
I smile, then, thinking of electricity,
leap up from my lawnchair and run
across the yard. "Oh, God," I shout.

"Look out! You'll be electrocuted."
But my neighbor only smiles, says,
"Don't worry, everything's waterproof."
And keeps mowing. Relieved I turn
and see my book of Zen lying face up
in the grass, soaked by rain.

Sleep

At 8:30 the neighbors up the hill
have turned out their lights.
After wind all day
it is calm. The kitchen fills
with the smell of garlic.
I am reading a book on memory,
wondering what is the connection
between the word *memory*
and the phrase *I remember*.
Noticing my left foot
wrap itself around my right,
I'm sure both have a life
separate from my own.
I look again and see the white socks
my father wore, his tense face
gone slack, his body lying on a couch
in front of a television.
Inside the socks his feet
are in constant motion
no matter how hard he sleeps.

Distance

Tomato as red as the sky.
Sliced open, out comes a rain of blue seeds
barely visible through the leaves.

Time's unwanted children – birthdays,
anniversaries, holidays celebrating
the memory of the dead in war.

Before the assembled townspeople
the VFW President steps forward and stands
in the sun, ready to speak.

Suddenly he wakes on a patch of grass
in Peace Park, Hiroshima, a sea of faces
around him, staring, as if at a corpse.

But no, he was only tired
after the long walk, his legs aflame,
and he lay down on the soft green grass,
the day all glittering light and gently warm.

Guatemala, the Year of Our Lord 1984

You try caressing whatever you touch
and it flies from you. You whisper
it back but it flies. Simultaneously
things come unbidden. The skin is a house
made of doors which do not lock, which,
in fact, have fallen from their hinges.
Passersby poke their heads in at will.
Some casually enter then just as casually
leave. I step across nails and bits of glass
to a white wicker chair. Securely seated
there is a cadaver – eyes, testicles
and hands removed, arms folded in lap
making the missing hands cover
the missing sex. In a chaise longue
facing this man is a woman,
her red fingernail polish intact
though her fingers have been severed
and have fallen to the floor. Someone's
dolly, a real dolly of cotton and rubber,
also lies on the floor, hair pulled out,
miniature plastic teeth and latex nipples
removed. I leave this room for the kitchen,
cluttered with last year's newspapers,
history now. Like an animal I sit down
to read and read about the house,
entered repeatedly by unknown armed men
who committed certain complicated acts
leaving behind a number of unidentifiable
bodies now strangers to even the householders.

I wish to report one story:
July 4, 1979, an unhappy coincidence,
a pregnant woman was found raped
on the front lawn. Her husband,
a campesino of indeterminate age,
lay near her, decapitated. His head
had been placed in her vagina, open eyes
gazing toward the world, serenely now
it would seem though that is an
unjustifiable assumption I poetically
make about the dead. The woman
had been cut open, her unborn infant
lifted from her and laid down
in front of her husband's head.
The infant's mouth had been filled
with gravel. My only defense
for telling you this is that it is true,
a weak defense indeed. But if you push
a series of needles through a person's tongue,
it becomes hard for that person to speak
and when finally the needles are removed,
it is nearly impossible. You are free
to leave the house. Get out!
Run now! Look at the strong young men
and clear-complexioned young women.
It does not matter if it is raining
or if the sun is out, the sky
may be as blue as an eye or filled
with racing clouds, the innumerable grays.
The breeze comes up and the leaves
begin to move, to sway on their delicate
stems. On the street as if awaiting
the first leaf's fall, the mammoth older
cars roll carefully from block to block.

Night after Night

There are galloping horses I do not ride.
I have ridden them all my life.
Now I stand and watch. The horses
throw their heads in the cold air,
their breath as visible as birds,
unclipped feathers in the wind. The horses
gallop through all my fields and hills.

I make love. I do not know if my lover
is male or female. I do not know
if I am female or male. I cannot decide
if I am afraid or desperately happy.

I give birth. The crown of my daughter's
head slips from me. She follows,
only to be a teenaged boy, lips blue
but hot, penis erect. Half inside me,
his body begins to tear mine. He does not
know speech but his eyes fill with tears.

I know how to fly. I have only one wing,
a wounded bird fallen from a branch.
The dog, so well trained, so gently
takes me in its mouth, carries me, loping
with hardly a catch in its cadence, home,
to the hunter. When the dog drops me
at its master's feet, I rise and fly,
one wing carrying me away.

Eating Dinner at My Sister's

It's another warm night.
The grass is growing.
The city shouts its city song.
The birds and bugs clack
and buzz, saying, "Here we are!"
How small the yard is
and how close the house
next door. House after house.

In the middle of our dinner
the atomic bomb falls.
For a moment I feel terror,
then, having waited so long,
this terror turns to relief.
I set down my dinner
and watch. Then I run
screaming in the yard.
Blinded, I collide with my sister
who takes my hand.

This close, what is left
of a person is shadow,
pale gray on a shattered wall
or dark on the dusty earth.

The rising mushroom spirals toward us.
My sister opens her mouth and swallows.
The moon rises and its cold light seems warm.
I slow my breathing to count the breaths:
one – do not flee adversity,

two – only good can come of facing fear,
three – a single pure soul
can save the earth.

I thank my sister for swallowing
our bomb and wonder how many
have done it before, how many
whose names I cannot say.

After Rain, a Warm Day in December

The grass is steaming and the woodpile, too.
My mother bends and brushes the hair
away from my face. I look up
and see the sun, a faint circle
around her head like the circle
around Christ's head in my Sunday school
primer. I am still in the warmth,
my mother beside me.

"I could sit like this forever," she says.
The cloud of breath that was her voice
floats there a moment then disappears.
"Trust people," my mother goes on,
"Assume they are exactly what they appear.
Assume no one is contaminated even if not pure."

Shining in that season, the sun
is impossible to ignore. We don't
need to build a fire. The torn tarp
covering our woodpile flaps in the breeze,
sounding like a small animal scraping at something
or a person working with a machine far away.

That is how these conversations
with my mother go. And that is
how the absent rain feels. And even
the thin winter sun. Warm,
but coming from far away –
as if the person working looks up
thinking the wind is someone
calling out a name.

Bukavu, Zaïre, the Word Love

Today I admit you are gone.
"Muzoki," I call in my foreign accent.
"Muzoki," I shout. For weeks
I have been looking wherever I go –
in the market among the Mamas,
guardians of groundnuts and rice
and glowing smoke that disappears;
around the men's plaza drinking
from long reed straws plunged
into fifty-five gallon drums
of banana beer, or sorghum;
hunched in a doorway, drunk
with soldiers, with cripples,
with blind children, with some
whose minds are dim, insinuating
your name; at the Catholic Relief stall
sniffing buttons and soaps,
torn blouses and dirty shirts.
I poke my fingers in places
from which they will never return.

The stink of dead animals,
in the market, always,
this stink of dead animals.

We walk away from that through eucalyptus,
the smell in our hair and on our skin.
For a moment we dance barefoot
in the pungent leaves.
I push my face deep in the curve

where your shoulder becomes your neck,
where the eucalyptus becomes you.
We both breathe deeply and the sun
pours down through the leaves,
mottling our skin with pools
of dark and light.

Blytheville, Arkansas, a Dance

I climb onto my bicycle and ride, day after
day, the cracking streets by Simmons Metalworks,
corrugated sheet metal walls
flapping in a heavy breeze, over
the railroad tracks, each crossing
a malignant explosion of asphalt and iron,
past the unusable NIBCO loading docks
where a truck backing down would settle
in three feet of still metallic water.
The Elm Street Market – Fresh Fish Daily,
We Accept Food Stamps – is closed for good.
Cemented into one wall a rusting fan
continues to turn, oblivious to the missing
motor. At Mac's Lounge, the men smoke
out front and at Jesse's Hay-Mac Disco –
"We sell ice by the bag and by the cup" –
it's the same. A teenage girl
steals a paper from Richard Lum's Store.
Down the road another girl dances
in the street, her fat mother next to her,
smiling, rocking on her delicate feet,
keeping time to the beat of her daughter's song.
The houses lining the street peel to
unpainted clapboard the color of rain.
Dark automobiles sink in muddy yards.
Metal chairs rest on sagging wooden porches.
In a flooded field the neighborhood dogs
run. A lactating bitch throws up white worms
and her pups eat the squirming gel. This
is a Black neighborhood in Blytheville.
I am another transient White like the postman

delivering a letter to a house he'll never enter
or the meter reader with his clipboard and tie
or the man from the oil company checking
the depth in the tank. When I roll by
I can hear the sky bend behind me
and the dancing girl's fingers
snapping like thunder. In Zaïre
this is how one calls to another.
"Citoyen!" one says with a snap,
"S'il vous plaît." To one's friends
the same snap but gentler word –
"T'es pas là?" And so happily lost
amid the dark faces I turn. But this
is not some village near Bukavu, Zaïre.
This is Blytheville, Arkansas, USA.
And the girl has stopped dancing.
And is walking away.

Kibuye, Rwanda, We Wave Goodbye

"Goodbye." I say in English
and we are both surprised. Doubly so
when he answers, "Urabeho." I would have thought
malaria or sleeping sickness or schistosomiasis
to have caused his departure.
That's what the Umuzungu fear –
careful not to walk in marshy water,
always spraying, spraying to kill mosquitos,
swallowing Nivaquine and Aralen. Yes,
I would have thought such to be our parting.
But the placement of weakness and strength
surprises even the construction engineers.
My young American steeled himself against
each possible disease, injecting gamma globulin
himself, pushing the needle through his skin,
the thick serum making the tissue bulge
and ache. Careful, he double boiled
his water then ran it through a filter.
Each Sunday, scant hours after swallowing
his Aralen tablet with this pure water,
this man would start to shake,
fever and chills for twenty-four hours,
a small malaria to keep him malaria free.
His eyes would fill with oily thick water.
He was unable to see. He hugged a blanket
around his body and clenched his jaws
until his teeth twisted in his head, seeming
to crack apart like clods. Serving him,
I watched and once touched his face,
my pale yellow palm across his even paler,

oddly smooth white forehead. It was bad,
but not so bad as to drive him away.
He smiled at me, seeming to say
you cannot tell in whose voice the Lord
will choose to speak. I say Lord
and mean many Gods, including the Christian
one, and a variety of spirits residing
in trees, goats and drops of water.
This is the late twentieth century
and even here we all live
in at least two worlds at once.
The voice resides in each possible
receptacle, even the most unlikely,
even the departing Umuzungu.
And speaks. In the end, it was speech,
I'm sure, that drove the young man away.
His more cynical compatriots, too. Those
who laugh not only at the voice in a goat,
but laugh also at the voice in their own
elderly tired God. Laughter
drove them to the Girunya Road,
to the airport in Kigali, Bukavu, Bujumbura.
There is an airport whichever way one turns
and another world to which one can fly,
leaving behind a variety of pests and voices,
the variety of ways each pest speaks
clearly of the place the one who is leaving
will forever remain.

My Father Explains How We Came Here

I always tried to stick with a job.
I figured you're not hurting anyone
but yourself when you quit.
Maybe something better will come along
if you're patient, maybe
you'll save $10,000.

One way or another lots of money
doesn't get to the people
who need it. We're in a recession
again. It'll probably get worse.
If you work for the Welfare
the more people who are on it
the better your chance of keeping your job.
In this world you buy food, clothing, shelter;
you buy everything. Beautiful days
make me glad to be alive.

Over the mines the yellow sun shines
in a sulphur dioxide sky.
The air is pickled red and blue.
It's hot. The papers call this Paradise.

It really is hot.
So many years since I've seen snow.
So little rain most plants don't have leaves.

I'm not disappointed.
I tried to save $10,000.
There might be another Depression.

I saw enough of the first one.
I had a family, had to make a living,
tried growing flowers. First winter
there was a power-out, thousands of begonias
froze in the cold greenhouse. I went into a rage,
breaking panes of glass, throwing clay pots to the floor.

I gave up the greenhouse,
went down to the river
and worked in the paper mill.
Later there was the plywood business.
Things just seemed to get worse.
Some weeks there wasn't any work at all.
$10,000 got further away. My hands
and shoulders were getting stiff.
When it rained I couldn't move.

That's when we came to the desert.
Put you kids in the car, everything else
in a U-Haul trailer and off we went.
The first summer the heat nearly killed me.
Worked in an aluminum mill. No union.
Arizona's a right-to-work state.
Right to starve. They call it free
choice, the rich.

I'd work three weeks and be laid off two,
work two and be off four. In between
I worked for sweatshop cabinet makers
in sheds with sheet metal roofs —
minimum wage, 110 degrees outside, hotter in,
woodchips and sawdust in my clothes
and hair. I always went back

when the aluminum mill called.
Guess I was glad to go back.

One year a trailer hitch snapped
while I was connecting it, fell
on my arms, crushed them. Doctors
wanted to take off my hands.
I said you do and I'll kill myself.
Now I've got both hands. Didn't work
for almost a year. Finally
I got on at the County. Never
had a job I liked. Don't expect
you will either. Evenings I sit
and count the days till I retire —
workdays, sickdays, holidays, paid
days of leave, 700, 699, 698. . . .
Some days I think it's working.

It still seems hot
and I'll always be a stranger.
I may die on this desert
but there's no way I can get myself born here.
I grow roses that burn in the sun.
I thin peaches.
I pick asparagus in April.
I keep on working. It's odd
how easy the days go by.

The Raspberry Canes

The raspberry canes stiffen and bend.
Mint leaves blacken and fall.
For the cottonwood it is not only leaves
but branches that plummet down,
striking the sturdy grass again and again.

Surprised by an October blizzard,
I step off the porch
and walk barefoot
through soft snow.

Shine

I lie on the white snow with the white clouds
above my face. The wind blows through
the hairs in my nose. It pushes
the clouds in a parade of blurry shapes:

a frozen horse, a drunken saguaro,
a chewed-up bone, the face of a drowned man,
a charging lion. The clouds
disappear and there's only blue sky,

the same blue as the blue car
my father waxed once a month
on even the hottest Arizona days,
turning a soft rag in his hardened hands.

As he worked a drop of water would fall.
"Rain?" he'd hope. Then he'd lean over
the shining surface, see the sweat fall
from his face to the paint, and smile.

At Home

My mother and I sit at home.
Our brown adobe house is low and the windows small.
Even on hot days my sister walks outside.
She climbs up on the flat roof and lies naked
in the sun. I go to watch but she
pulls the ladder up and shoos me away.
Where the ladder bumps the wall,
a little dirt crumbles to the ground.

Nearby houses look like ours but if I squint
they look like clumps of sage
or rocks along an arroyo.
When the wind blows the earth swirls up
in great beige clouds. I go inside.

The house is dark and cool. My mother
sits in a chair near a window. She looks
out to see the sea, a vast memory
the open desert helps her hold. My father
comes home from work tired and hot.
Sweat drips from his browned body.
He drinks water from the tap,
walks into the bedroom, removes his shoes,
and lies down. How plain these rooms are!
My mother's eyes shine with moisture.
I can hear my father breathing
in the other room. I fold my hands
on my lap and dream of the future.

Blue Ice, My Grandmother's Story

It was winter. Each afternoon my sisters and I
went to skate. The ice was so clear it was blue.
One day we came home, our cheeks burning red,
and our father lined us up in the living room.

He aimed his rifle at us. He called us names —
words I did not know. He said he'd shoot us
dead if we moved. He swayed on one foot. "Dead,"
he said. If we moved. "One by one," he said.

The harder I tried to stand still the more I felt
myself spinning round and round, sure I'd fall.
I began to cry and my sisters held me. Our mother
stood in the doorway. She trembled as the gun

came round to her. She talked him out of it
and, dizzy, I fell to the floor. All of us girls
grew up. All of us married. All of us had children
and grew old. When he died we went to his funeral.

In that room I cannot say what color the wallpaper was.
Maybe red or gray. I cannot remember what color
his eyes were. Perhaps green or brown. I do know.
It was winter and we skated, the ice so clear it was blue.

Kiev, the Ukraine, Nuclear Accident

In the world we've made
a cloud approaches Wyoming,
a radioactive cloud born in a fire,
a graphite fire in a nuclear power plant
gone wrong. The fire will not stop.

For three days it has been raining.
In Oregon people are advised not to drink rainwater.
And in Washington and Idaho. Here in Buffalo, Wyoming,
our town water comes from Clear Creek flowing
down out of the Bighorn Mountains
and through the center of town,
beside the Busy Bee Cafe,
under the bridge on Main Street.
The rain falls, the water flows.
All the water that can makes its way
to the creek out of which we drink.

I sigh and with that sigh I am a child
standing face up in a heavy rain –
southern Arizona, the dark sky, the water tumbling
from the foreign clouds and sluicing along
a gutterless street. My eyes are closed
so I feel the drops pelt my eyelids.
My mouth is open as wide as I can open it,
tongue hanging out. The rain pounds
on my tongue but does not hurt.

I love this feeling and, as my mouth fills,
I swallow – cool water on what, thirty minutes before,

was another hot day. I let my arms rise
away from my sides and I begin to turn,
to spin in place like the blades of a propeller,
or those seeds with wings that come down from the trees
like eggbeaters upside down, or a ballet dancer
I have never seen. The water flies off
the ends of my fingers as it continues
to strike my tongue. Around and around
until I am so dizzy I fall and lie on my back,
eyes still closed, mouth still open. My mother
comes out in the yard to watch the rain.
She speaks to me and I look at her.
She smiles. Then she lies down next to me.
Side by side on our backs we both close our eyes,
open our mouths and drink the rain
that goes on falling.

The Soviet Street Named for the Poet Osip Mandelstam

The nineteenth century Russian poet Batyushkov,
while walking down a St. Petersburg street,
was stopped by a stranger who politely inquired
as to the time. "What is the time?" Batyushkov
repeated. "The time is eternity." A long time.

Early in our century the poet Mandelstam wrote
that the loftiness of Batyushkov's reply
was base. Not many years later, after having
accused Joseph Stalin of murdering peasants,
Mandelstam was arrested. Released. Rearrested.

Mandelstam was last reported scavenging food
from the garbage heap of a transit camp
near Vladivostok. That was December 1938.
Now we have Mandelstam's poems which come to us
from hiding – from saucepans and old shoes.

Mandelstam's wife was named Nadhezhda.
That is a beautiful name. So is Elizabeth,
Virginia, Teresa, Marisol, Ann. Perhaps
your wife bears one of these names and your name
is Samuel, Boris, Miguel or John.

Nadhezhda memorized Osip's poems. She says
he wrote that he too would create beauty
"from cruel weight . . ." and that he wondered
wherein lay his guilt when the delicate stars
struck him only as milky, not distant.

Mandelstam believed his words carried the aftertaste
of misfortune and smoke. Misfortune and smoke,
the aftertaste of much death. Batyushkov
has been dead so long, and Stalin too now is dead.
Only the stranger's question about time remains.

I do not know if anyone has ever been right
about anything. Stalin was cruel, Mandelstam
was cold, Batyushkov was flip. In mourning death
we naturally mourn life and I felt sad when told
there is no street in Russia named Osip Mandelstam.

Flight

My mother says the angels don't know night
from day. They open and close doors, they
poke their boneless heads and bodies out
and squint into the atmosphere.

Just as we, they'd like to know,
but they surrender nothing.
Their arms wave round, their flesh
folds like brown hills in early spring,

their wings are sharp
like the wings of cranes and they knife
through rooms in which they never sit –
our living room – filled with snow and mist.

The rivers run back and forth. If only
we heard the water change direction,
that would tell us light from dark.
There are plenty of clues: the tides,

the phases of the moon, leaves that fall
and reappear, the cranes who nest and fly.
And say there's no difference
between a heron and a crane.

Or between the scream of a frog impaled
and a man snoring. Any two things different
can be shown to be alike. The old sun
calls and together we rise, happily, into day.

Bamboo

All morning the bamboo rattles in the breeze.
In the afternoon I hear a plane overhead.
Later I hear a boom. For a moment
I think a nuclear bomb has been dropped.
After the first bomb there will be another
and after the shock a wave of fire,
what the Japanese called Unforgettable
Fire. For me and for most everyone
I know this will be the end – ten million,
sixty million, two hundred million dead.
The government calls it "megadeath"
and says even if two hundred million
die, that's not everyone.

A Jewish doctor who survived the Holocaust
says that for survivors of the blast
bone marrow blood cell production will stop.
In two weeks these people will begin to vomit
and bleed to death. Another boom
interrupts my thoughts. I shiver.
A convulsive snap runs down my spine.
It fades and the plane flies away.

I take a sheet of paper and try
to write this poem but it's hard
to concentrate while the bamboo
rattles outside my darkened window.

Glendive, Montana, the Old Bridge

The things that endure are those we neglect,
so I am thankful
when no one cares for what I love.

The Lord is a woman.
None of us has a right to speak
of the secret places of his body.

Prayer is God's voice whispered to itself –
the flight of the alone to the alone.
God is some foreign language for "I am."

No one need believe anything.
Each life is a trip through Paradise.
It's a tough trip.

The water in the river is low and fast.
Along the shore a teen-aged boy
plays the saxophone for a teen-aged girl.

Soon the snow in the mountains will melt
and the river will swell.
It will become a flood.

The faraway cities are leaden
with bad air and despair
and money.

In the distance behind a butte
I cannot see, cattle are bawling.
The wind blows their voices to me.

Strange streets and unfamiliar roads,
planets I have not yet seen.
I wave and the bridge begins to sway.

Butare, Rwanda, at the Market

"Vive la Révolution Rwandaise"
reads the phrase under the president's face –
Habyarimana Juvenal, a military man seen
on yellow T-shirts throughout the land,
a man we treat with respect though here
in the country of the poor there is no shame
in wearing the president's face
until it is tattered and torn.

Just so is Juvenal worn
over the breasts and stomach
of the fattest woman I've ever seen.
She sits on the earth
roasting and selling groundnuts,
hers an honorable profession
among the few left to choose.

Her breasts fill the president's cheeks,
making them puff out like a squirrel's
so full of nuts it cannot carry them all,
but unwilling to give up and let some fall.

It makes me smile and when I do,
the impossibly large woman claps her hands
causing her breasts to bounce
and Juvenal's face to contort.
Her stomach tightens making
his mouth pinched and tight,
unable to talk or issue commands.

All due respect and
Vive la Révolution Rwandaise!
We smile and laugh
and she hands me a paper cone
of roasted nuts. I pay fifty francs,
say, "Urakoze cyane, Mama,"
and walk away, eating my fill.

Summer, 1970, Rich and Poor

My classmates are in Vietnam.
They make sweeps across the delta
while I make $2.20 an hour
in a ski-pole factory and sweep
up at day's end, going home
to wait and sleep.

My foreman Jimmy's a Vietnam vet.
Sweating in the afternoon heat,
he glides around back to smoke
among the stacks of long white
cardboard boxes that hold
the silent poles, cool and clean.

While I hammer a plug into an aluminum tube,
Jimmy talks to me through the wall.
"You know how far Vietnam is from here?"
"How far?" I ask, though I know the answer.
"About as far as rich from poor. Or as far
as a body bag from a cardboard box."

When a higher-up walks by
I whistle and out comes Jimmy.
He does the same for me.
He reminds me we are protecting
us from them. Once I stole
a dozen pairs of poles and sold
them to friends. I told myself
I needed the money. But there are poor
people everywhere and I was not so poor.

Jimmy told me a story about a thief
who ransacked a poor man's house,
tearing things apart and taking
what little there was of value.
When the poor man returned
it was too dark to see
until a cloud drifted away
revealing the moon. The man
who had lost everything noticed
the moon in the window and smiled.

"Think about it," Jimmy said.
And I did.

On the Bus Riding to You

"You don't have to make love
to everyone you love," you'd said,
and I'd agreed but now, with you gone,
I wish we had.

The windows rattle, shake loose your absent voice.
It rolls around in my head
as the bus rolls down the road.

"There is a position each of us
is afraid to be put in."

"A friend who has died is closer
to home than one who has simply moved."

All your pregnant sayings.
I write them on a scrap of paper.
The old man next to me leans over
to ask if I am a student. I smile
to think that in my middle thirties
I can look so young. "No," I say,
"I'm just writing." And the man turns
to talk to another old man across the aisle.

"Forty-six years of work,"
the one who spoke to me says,
"I don't begrudge a man what little
good in the end may come to him. . . ."
Both wear wedding bands
tight on swollen fingers

but neither is with his wife.
"I took the Civil Service Exam,
got it all right
and they hired someone else.
Isn't that the way."

His age and way of talking
remind me of your Swedish aunt,
the time she took off her heavy
stockings and you saw her white skin,
whiter than you believed possible,
and you stared – your black eyes,
black hair, Filipino skin.

Once you told me we must all watch
what we say, but especially if our friend
is a poet – for when a poet's your friend,
your every secret may end up written down
for all the world to see. I assured you
no one much reads poems.

You went on, saying, "Just don't
demean me. Don't put me back
in the Philippines or in a nursing home
or all day at a sink washing dishes."
Now I would put you anywhere
but where you are.

I shake my head and return
to my reflection in the window,
the two old men telling their lives,
the bus rolling down the road to you,
making the trees seem to flash as we pass.

Another Bus, Coming Home

The young man leans over
the side of the seat bringing his mouth
close to the singing girl's ear.

"Sounds like y'all having a good time."

No answer.

"Oh, man, why y'all quit singing?"

He leans farther to speak
to the second girl silent
in the window seat.

"Where y'all from?
Y'all from Yakima?
I just come from Yakima. Hell,
that place is dead. Where's
the happening spot in that town?"

Pointing to her seatmate,
the second girl says, "Her place."
And laughs, then, "Oh, Christ,
I brought it on myself, I really
did, brought it on myself."
The young man tries the first girl again.

"What's yer name?"

And again no answer.

"Oh, man, you afraid?
Whatchu afraid of? I won't hurt you."

And to the second girl,

"Tell yer friend I ain't gonna hurt her."

"She's not my friend, she's my sister."

"Yer sister?"

One girl's white, the other's black.
The white one turns, says,
"Yeah, she's adopted." Laughing,
the black one says, "Naw, she's adopted."
Then each gives the other
a kiss on the cheek.
"We sisters."

Hesitation, then

"Hey, you . . . I mean . . . y'all not . . . ?"

One girl says, "We always kiss each other."
And the other asks, "Don't you kiss your sister?"

The young man retreats to the back
of the bus to drink beer and try
to smoke cigarettes without the driver seeing,
but the driver does, and stops him.
And the two girls sing out loud
and laugh all the way to Seattle.

Laugh, 1943

On my tenth birthday
my father says, "Feel of this,"
and takes my index finger in his hand.
He brings it to his right eye
and makes me touch his face.
My finger slides along the hard
sharp surface. I pull away.
He laughs, drops my hand.
"Steel plate," he says,
"Holds the eye in my head."

Now I stand at my father's door.
He lies still in bed,
both eyes closed. His face
is moist. A little cloud of breath
rises from his mouth. With each exhalation
there is a crackle in his throat
like applause following a laugh.
He's got a cold. In '43 he had a cold.
Like most plastic surgery patients
he might have died of pneumonia
while new skin replaced old.

World War II, Jap fighters,
the humid hospital, the Asian kids
down the block are just kids.
I don't know how pneumonia works
and I don't speak when my father
tells how it feels
to have your face removed.

But my mouth falls open
and my father laughs again, seems
happy. Outside, I lift a hand
to my face, touch the skin
below the eye and draw a line.
My father's laugh follows it
through the day.

Sitka, Alaska, Hidden Faces

Above me the flag drowses on a still day,
gold stars on a night-blue sky.
Behind the fishing boats, dredge and fill,
two tennis courts as if this were
Poughkeepsie or some suburb of L.A.,
Any-old-where, the thunk-thunk-thunk
of a fluorescent yellow ball against a racket.
The fishing boats laze, waiting for evening,
for exit. The Princess Something-or-Other
fills the bay. Visiting tourists step ashore
and into the woods, mildly pleased to stand
where Tlingits and Russians stood, to smell
the exotic past of Sitka, a small town in Alaska.
On the rocks there is moss, this green going to gray.
Along the beach seaweed dries among stones
and driftwood. A tiny yellow flower blooms.
Its five tongue-shaped petals are broad paddles
slapping air. Perfect, I think,
then notice bits missing, as if bites
had been taken by some hungering insect.
The sky is blue – one of the ordinary twelve
clear days here each summer. A fly lands on my leg
and walks among the hairs, high above my skin.
There's a hum far away which could be
the garbage-burning plant or the sea or my breath.
Close to me, but out of sight, a Tsimshian man
is carving a cedar pole, revealing the faces
the pole carries within – Raven and Bear,
Wolf and Whale, the beings within beings
until the carver himself appears

with his tools and the steady sound of steel
on wood, the hard easing into the soft, the pulse
which wakes me and I turn to face
the carver, the hammer and adze,
the standing tree, one world and another,
inside both of which we live.

Fire

We rode together in the car, Grandma and me,
coming home in the middle of the night.
I saw a glow in the sky like sunrise
but it came from the west. I was all turned
around and lost track of time.

"Don't be frightened," Grandma said,
"It's a logging yard on fire. The sun
will still come up where it should."
The night sky, the forest all around, the glowing logs.
It was both miracle and tragedy.

We drove close enough to see
and helped roll a burning car
down an embankment into a river. It hit
the water and went dark in a hiss of steam.
We were happy but someone had lost a car.

After that, Grandpa died and Grandma was alone.
Nights she'd sit up by the stove, dozing,
then rise to feed the fire, pacing
around the room. The opposite of a moth
at a lightbulb, Grandma was a light
circling the dark death of her husband.

One night her cotton nightgown touched
the cast iron stove and started to burn.
She woke, beat at the flames then fell
to the floor. I was the one who found her,
tried to wake her, looked around, called

to my mother, cried, remembered to check
for a pulse and reached for her hand.
Where I touched her the skin came off onto my own.

All those fires are one. When I walk
outside at night, I see the stars
as light from fires that went out
long ago. The logging yard comes back
to me – part tragedy, part miracle.
I have to believe that when so much
is lost, there's also something gained.

Farm Accident

A tractor fell on her brother James,
whose name I rarely say, leaving
my mother to play the eldest son.
And though I was her first born
it was another daughter she raised.

I had the same rights as a boy.
"You must accept responsibility," she'd say,
"For your life; you must control your life. Though
you do what pleases you, never waste your talent.
No matter what you think you want,
later on you'll want something else."

I was a boy. She was a woman. It was the spring
of 1951. The fields got wet and hard to work.
The tractor stuck and though the wheels stopped,
the worm drive kept turning and the tractor rose,
falling backwards on itself, the field and James.

At the funeral the Lutheran minister spoke calmly.
James once spoke like this, asking whether God
and the angels were male or female. And the minister
thought and calmly answered back that no,
they had no sex. And you couldn't tell
if either James or the minister were joking.

People say I do things like a woman,
and my mother, they say, is something
like a man. Possibly James would know
if this makes the two of us more
like God and the angels, or less so.

Yuma, Arizona, the Harvest

I walk slowly into a field
of cantaloupe, bend and begin to pick.
At noon, I straighten and walk home.
These fields and these streets –
all my life and still they are strange.
The birds whistle above my head
in the language of the trees.
At my feet, the hungry dogs
growl in the tongues of their owners.
At first my dreams were in English,
then, as a student, in Spanish.
Now I don't remember.
Mt. Baboquivari rises to the northeast,
the sacred mountain of the Papago.
Lightning dances on the red horizon
and rain falls. After lunch I walk
back to work, to make the harvest.
I look at the fence dividing Arizona
from Sonora, the United States from Mexico.
It's a tall fence. In the sun's afternoon
glare the bits of plastic garbage stuck
in the chain link glow and flutter
like the petals of bright flowers.

Chihuahua, One Meteorologically Strange January

It's ten degrees out in the capital.
In my room it's thirty-six. If it'll burn,
we burn it – wood, kerosene, garbage, oil.
The earth under a white sheet, the sky
is the only brown thing left. At midday
I'm in bed fully dressed, six cotton blankets
over me, my clean shirts over that.
I open the shutter and look out, squinting
into the pearl light, snow still coming down.

A Tarahumara woman walks
down from the Sierra, alone in a place
whose language she does not speak.
Shoeless, the white soles of her wide
brown feet slap the slushy stones.
On her back, eyes wide open, her baby
is tied in a bundle of white cloth.
In the cold wind, her flaring layered skirts
whirl – yellow and green and rose.

Those Days

When we met, Emeritus Professor
Ernest Kuhl was already old.
Now he has died. In those days
I was driving cab –
three days a week from six
to six, morning to night,
long hot days. The rest
of the week I was a student.
Every morning the professor
prepared lunch for two, carefully
placing it in a wicker basket
with a red and white checked cloth
as cover. Then he put on his jacket,
straightened his bow tie
and awaited his cab.
The first day I was late,
lost, unsure if I should ascend
the long drive to the house.
Finally he walked out to me,
complaining and hot. He slapped
the yellow hood of the car.
I drove to a nursing home
where he had lunch with his wife.
On the return trip he explained
he could not take care of himself
and of her, too. He was sorry.
"We have lunch. The food they serve
would make anyone want to die."
Soon he asked for me by name.
I'd drive to the door,

walk in the kitchen for the basket
and help the professor into the cab.
I was young, longhaired,
studying to be a poet. "You can't
learn to be a poet," he'd scowl,
"The university is a home for scholars
not artists." One day, almost
Fourth of July, he showed me
two ripe ears of corn, perfect
even rows. "Each kernel,"
he said, "An Iowa pearl."
He started the plants indoors
then moved them outside
when it warmed up – ripe corn
by the Fourth, a surprise
for his wife. Every year
this surprise for her.
He laughed and laid the corn
on the table. Then, picking up
two stemmed glasses, he led me
downstairs to the dark
earthen basement and a wall
of bottles, picking one out.
"This is the last I have,"
he said, "an 1888 Madeira
given me by a colleague in 1935."
He meant to open it and offer
me a drink. I said I couldn't,
it wouldn't be right. He laughed
at my conservatism as he opened
the bottle, an ordinary day
for no reason to celebrate
a holiday left unnamed.

He poured some out, that 1888
Madeira, and we walked upstairs
into the light and there
the two of us, blinded, together
by the cab, we drank.

All through November

All through November it rained
and the ground was like a man
who thinks he is nothing.
At first it sank in
and the earth was soft and green.
As it went on, the water
lay in puddles. The man
went door to door, first to friends,
later to strangers, asking,
"How does it feel to be something?"
The friends' faces hardened,
the strangers' went slack.

The man asked to see
family photos, to know
what people had eaten for dinner,
what they bought on credit
and what they paid for with cash.
Anything would do.
Had he gone on he'd have ended
with the police or social workers.
Instead he went home
and looked at his face in the mirror.
He pulled up his shirt
and touched the scar near his rib
where he'd lain down on a piece of glass.

It was years ago
yet the scar was still warm.
His eyes brightened.

The more he looked at his body,
the more he was quiet.
He sat in a chair by himself
and hummed all through the night.

It was like his childhood
when all night the sea
would hum to him and in the morning
his father would bring his small boat
in from fishing and walk home.
His father's friend, who lived alone,
would unload whatever they'd caught.
And so the father came home
to have breakfast with his son
and bring the smell of the sea.

Alone now, the man
closed his eyes and slept,
a blanket covering his lap.
Like the sea, he kept humming.
There's no other man, is there?
No other man to be.

Life Story

"Old dreams do not die,"
a man tells me
and a woman walking by
says to another,
"I could smell rose water
on his hands."
Voices fade. I turn back
to something about a love
but I've missed it.
My cotton pants are thin,
the back of my shirt rises
from my waist as if
to take itself off.
Looking at my hands
I think a person
can do anything.
"Anything," I say aloud
and the man smiles,
looks away. He says,
". . . the old woman
who lived near us,
the one who drew water
from the well. I saw her
on the road and ran.
A crowd of boys circled
round and jeered, shouting
her name. When I could
take it no more, I ran
back to the road
and looked at her.

She removed her eye
and waved it at the screaming
boys who scattered
like dried leaves.
The woman came up to me,
put the eye in my hand.
It was glass.
I gave it back.
She pushed my hands together
to form a cup and poured
out a little water for me.
I took a drink.
She said something
in another language.
I think she made a blessing
but it could have been anything,
anything at all. . . ."
Listening to the story
of his life, my own
disappears. The sky
comes into the room
and a breeze blows
through our hair.
The man takes his wallet
from his pocket
and opens my hand,
placing in the palm
a foreign bill,
two folded receipts,
and a pale green ticket stub.
I look up confused.
He takes my hand again
and lifts the stub
from the damp palm, says,

"This is all there is,
almost nothing."
I look down, fingers curl
into a tiny bowl
filled with water.
But I can't hold it,
and that evening, alone,
other lives fill the room.
The earth is a life,
and the sea, the chair
on which I sit. Everyone
has gone home but I stay,
turn on the light
and read the story
of someone else's life:
a man coming toward me
on a road, far away,
a pale dot that could be
anything, anything.